THE SEARCH FOR THE TRUTH OF GOD

BY JOHN TERRELL AND JACK GAULT

Published by:

HAYES PRESS Publisher, Resources & Media,

The Barn, Flaxlands

Royal Wootton Bassett

Swindon, SN4 8DY

United Kingdom

www.hayespress.org

Unless otherwise indicated, all Scripture quotations are from the Revised Version Bible (Public Domain).

Table of Contents

PREFACE

THE ORIGINS OF ANY movement or organisation tend to become progressively obscured with the passage of the years. "One generation goeth and another generation cometh", and those who inherit a legacy of biblical truth and teaching can easily drift away from a clear understanding of the work of God which laid the foundation.

This could easily happen with the Churches of God today, so a reminder of important events a century ago, which we believe to have been a movement of the Holy Spirit, seems timely for younger people in these Churches today, including many whose parents and grandparents lived that much nearer to the events of which we write. It should also be useful and stimulating of thought, we hope, for many fellow-Christians who look around them with some dismay at modern trends in church unity movements and who wish to discover an assured scriptural way, a divinely given pattern, for corporate Christian service.

With these purposes in mind this book has been prepared, the revised successor of an earlier publication also entitled 'The Search for the Truth of God', but now out of print. Disciples in the Churches of God will, we trust, find here a factual review of the events leading to the establishing of the movement to which they belong; and a confirmation of its scriptural soundness. To disciples of the Lord Jesus who are unfamiliar with the Churches of God, the doctrinal approach in this booklet may in some respects seem surprising and will, we hope, prove challenging. For instance, the use of the term 'Churches of God' is different from the much wider application often given to 'Church' and 'Churches'. It is hoped that all our readers will earnestly search the Scriptures as the Beroeans did (Acts 17:10,11) to see whether these things are so. We believe that many Christians will do this in the same spirit of mutual love and respect which has prompted the writing of the book.

We are sure that readers will appreciate that many statements are made in these pages about scriptural doctrines which the authors could not immediately digress to justify from Scripture. The flow of the historical narrative would hardly allow of this, even if the statements sometimes seem to call for it. It is therefore important to draw attention to the Appendix where a summary of the teachings of the Churches of God is set out; and to the bibliography of literature of the Churches of God which deals at greater length with subjects such as 'Elders and the Elderhood' and our understanding of 'The Faith'. The Churches of God in the Fellowship of the Son of God, the Lord Jesus Christ, understand the motives of fellow believers who seek more accommodating ways of bringing Christians together in united spiritual service.

This publication makes clear that the eternal unity of the Church the Body of Christ is not in dispute. We are "members one of another" (Eph.4:25) through faith in our Lord Jesus Christ. Certain questions do, nonetheless, call for an answer in this matter of unity. Do we look for it at the expense of doctrine, or do we prayerfully seek out the way of the New Testament Churches in the Word of God? Whether the Kingdom of God has a clear *constitution* in the New Testament (Matt.28:19,20; Acts 1:3; 2:41,42) as well as a beautifully portrayed character (Rom.14:17) is also a question which requires an answer. And, can the case really be made that the House of God in our day includes all believers; or, is the building of the stones, living stones, of 1 Peter 2:5 a vital process, involving human responsibility, to be followed according to New Testament example and precept? These and related questions are here addressed. It is the prayer of those who have prepared this booklet, that it will lead to much heart concern on such issues; and it is offered in faith that its positive purpose will be fulfilled in God's grace and goodness.

JOHN TERRELL, JACK GAULT

INTRODUCTION

―――

IT IS ALMOST 125 YEARS since a movement among evangelical Christians, which we believe was of the Holy Spirit, led to the reestablishment of Churches of God linked together to form the Fellowship of the Son of God, the Lord Jesus Christ (comment on this designation, based on 1 Corinthians 1:9, will be found in the Appendix). These Christians separated themselves from companies of Christian Brethren for reasons which have not always been clearly understood, and have been much criticised. Those reasons have been explained in past publications of the Churches of God but some of these are now out of print. It therefore seems timely to re-state some of the events which took place in the early days of the Christian Brethren assemblies, for it is against this background that the reasons for separation to form Churches of God can be best understood. We believe this review will be especially helpful to present-day disciples in the Churches of God, enabling them to appreciate more fully the origins of the Fellowship of which they are a part. Christians not associated with these Churches may also, it is hoped, find the review informative and, perhaps, challenging.

What then is this movement and what were its origins? Do these origins and the main principles adhered to by the Churches of God really justify their existence in a world where Christians long for greater unity in witness to a non-Christian, or a 'post-Christian', world? What part can they play in the spread of the gospel of Christ and of the Kingdom of God? Can their relationship to other Christian denominations and their pattern of collective service be justified from the New Testament Scriptures? Since some of the truths which are dearly held among them tend to be regarded with a measure of reserve by other Christians, how best can the Churches of God interest others in these important matters?

An attempt is made in the following pages to answer some of these questions. As indicated above, over the years the Churches of God have produced numerous publications setting out the truths which they believe should direct Christians in their collective service and worship. Some of these are listed at the end of this book and deal with major matters such as the basic doctrines of the Churches of God, and their understanding of what the New Testament teaches about the Church which is the Body of Christ. An appreciation of the essential characteristics of the Church the Body of Christ, as distinct from those of Churches of God, is vital to our understanding of collective Christian service today. Companion publications deal with some of the fundamental issues surrounding collective Christian service generally. Examples are: 'The Faith'; 'The Holy Spirit and the Believer'; 'The Breaking of the Bread'; and 'Elders and the Elderhood'.

In addition the quarterly teaching magazine of the Churches of God, 'Needed Truth', endeavours to present a balanced diet of scriptural truth while maintaining a consistent witness to the basic issues of church doctrine which gave rise to Churches of God in collective testimony in modern times. It is our prayer that the contents of this publication will prove to be complementary to our other publications and of real help to many Christians, whether in the Churches of God today, or others interested in their origins and teachings. A summary of these teachings is given in the Appendix.

The purpose of this book is not, however, to repeat in detail the teaching set out in those other works. We shall concentrate rather on the historical roots of the Churches of God; why and how they came into existence; and the spiritual struggles of men and women who felt compelled to separate themselves on principles which they understood to be clear and unmistakable in the Word of God, and which could not be set aside.

It is a story of sadly differing convictions among believers, despite their common love for the One who claimed their lives and loyalty at Calvary. It is, we believe, a climax in the history of the recovery of truth which began so dramatically with the Reformation. There was a gradual shedding of the unscriptural practices and doctrines of the Roman Catholic Church, and a progressive recovery of divine truths as the Holy Scriptures became more widely available.

It is perhaps particularly appropriate to re-examine briefly this historical process at a time when many voices in the Christian world are prepared to question the very basis of the Reformation and its necessity. The broad ecumenical movement today seems ready to discard some of the most fundamental doctrines in the interest of unity. At the very root of it all is the issue of the authority and inerrancy of Holy Scripture and it is no accident that one of the most recent publications of the Churches of God, 'The Bible - its Inspiration and Authority', deals with this very subject. It is central to an understanding of God's will for His people and vital to the recognition of a divine pattern of service for disciples of the risen Christ who said:

> "All authority hath been given unto Me in heaven and on earth. Go ye therefore, and make disciples of all the nations, baptising them into the name of the Father and of the Son and of the Holy Spirit: teaching them to observe all things whatsoever I commanded you: and lo, I am with you alway, even unto the end of the world" (Matt.28:18-20).

It is our prayer that the contents of this publication will prove to be complementary to our other publications and of real help to many Christians, whether in the Churches of God today, or others interested in their origins and teachings. A summary of these teachings is given in the Appendix.

CHAPTER ONE: THE WAY LOST

———

IT IS OUR BELIEF THAT the apostolic teaching, given in the Acts of the Apostles and in the Epistles, is the only foundation upon which Christians should build today. In tracing the departure from this teaching which led to the declension of the first century it is necessary to examine briefly some of its causes.

The Book of Revelation was probably written about AD 94. This book is associated mainly with the apostle John's visions of heavenly things and of future events in God's unfolding purposes, but it is sometimes forgotten that the Revelation given to John was primarily for the seven Churches which were in Asia (Rev.1:4). Each of these Churches received an individual message of divine assessment, encouragement and warning, entirely appropriate to its condition.

The conclusion seems inescapable that, at the time of writing, only seven Churches were acknowledged by the Lord in the province of Asia, although there must at an earlier time have been more Churches than seven in that province, e.g. that at Colossae. In the middle of the second century AD the heroic and devout Polycarp was designated 'Bishop of Smyrna' and was clearly holding a governing role in a wide chain of Churches. When John wrote the Revelation, however, the Holy Spirit sent His Word to only seven. The wide spectrum of spiritual condition revealed in the messages to the seven Churches in chapters 2 and 3 indicates a serious risk of some of these 'lampstands' soon being removed from God's recognition unless spiritual cleansing and reviving took place. It may well be that such Churches, though no longer enjoying the acknowledgement of the Lord, would continue to prosper numerically, but at a terrible price. There was extensive departure from those New Testament practices, based on apostolic teaching, which had provided the foundation for the Churches of God and their united fellowship of service.

The Light Goes Out

The process of deterioration continued and serious liberties were taken, in particular with the apostolic principles of church constitution and government. The divine ordinances of Baptism and the Breaking of the Bread were 'developed' into practices barely recognisable when compared with the clear directions of the Lord and His apostles. At the same time the fundamental doctrines touching salvation and service were corrupted beyond recognition.

It needs to be remembered that by no means all of those church leaders (though responsible for this movement away from New Testament principles) were spiritual charlatans, self-seekers, or people making the Way a source of material gain. Doubtless many soon fell into such categories, but in the early centuries following the death and resurrection of the Lord devout men and women stand out in the record of history whose personal devotion to their Master was unassailable. Some paid for this with their lives. Even such very worthy people, however, had gradually come to fall in with practices and teachings which they must have known to be widely divergent from what Christ and His apostles taught.

The idea of continual historical development of doctrines and practice, and the adjustment of scriptural precept and example to 'fit' a later period of time, evidently became increasingly accepted. After the completion of the New Testament canon of Scripture, many unscriptural divergences from it arose and heresies developed, some of which are less immediately relevant than others to the modern history of Churches of God. They are nonetheless destructive of a sound body of biblical teaching and have proved disastrous both for individuals and for communities of professing Christians. Examples of these errors are the establishment of holy days and feast days; of celibacy and monastic orders; the excessive accumulation of church properties, buildings and lands; and an attitude to warfare and military service which the early Fathers wholly deprecated.

Other issues of more direct importance to our main consideration arose in the early centuries AD and errors developed from which the road back has been long and painful. With regard to baptism, the practice of infant sprinkling is a prime example of corruption, as is also the distortion of the Breaking of the Bread. The process of deterioration which took place in the observance of these two ordinances, the only two for which there is New Testament authority, will be reviewed first of all.

Baptism

Baptism features in the New Testament principally in two forms. Firstly there is the baptism of the believer in the Holy Spirit (1 Cor.12:13), and the sealing with the Divine Spirit (Eph.1:13) both of which take place at the time of the new birth. Secondly, there is disciple baptism by immersion in water, an outward sign of the inward grace received at conversion.

Now we know from the Acts of the Apostles that baptism by immersion of believers into the Divine Name was practised by the early Churches who took up the Great Commission of Matthew 28 in establishing the Christian community. Before the end of the second century AD, regeneration was being linked to physical water baptism. Around the year 200 AD Tertullian wrote: "... the act of baptism, itself carnal in that we are plunged in water, has a spiritual effect in delivering us from our sins a man descends into the water and, being immersed, with the utterance of a few words rises up out of it scarcely if at all cleaner in body but - incredible consequence - the possessor of eternal life."

Incredible consequence indeed - certainly if the Master's teaching and the practice of His apostles are to retain their credibility! But now it was only a few steps to infant sprinkling, which was widely recognised by the 6th century AD. So, unbelieving adults came to rely on baptism, rather than faith in Christ, as the means of their salvation; and infants were sprinkled unto eternal life; both constituting error with the most far-reaching and disastrous consequences. Remnants of this obvious setting aside of scripture truth persists even in late stages of the restoration of truth in modern times.

The Breaking of the Bread

Truth relating to the Breaking of the Bread was compromised at an early stage. The simple ceremony commanded by the Lord to the apostles and observed week by week (Acts 20:7) became corrupt both in its nature and meaning. By the time of Tertullian an unscriptural priestly function had arisen for a very select few. The 'Remembrance' became a sacrifice and the table an altar so that by the end of the 3rd century AD the early simplicity and preciousness were gone. To receive the emblems of the Master's body and blood came to be regarded as life-giving and the bread and wine themselves as 'transubstantiated' into the literal body and blood of Christ. It is little wonder that when centuries later, God-fearing men and women recognised the enormity of the heresies that had developed, the 'Remembrance' found a central place in the restoration process.

Church Rule and Government

Another important departure from the doctrine of the Lord developed in the matter of the care of the Churches. The appointment of elders to tend the flock of God in apostolic times is clearly recorded. The terms which appear in the epistles-elders, overseers and bishops-all refer to the same office (Acts 20:17-28; Titus 1:5,7; 1 Pet. 5:1,2). Such men were recognised and appointed in each of the early New Testament Churches of God (Acts 14:23). The characteristics and qualifications of elders are set out very plainly in the Word (1 Tim. 3:1-7; Titus 1:5-9). Shepherd care, teaching and exemplary personal and home life were paramount. These men were the pastors and administrators of the Churches.

As time went on, however, a change began to take place and one elder became elevated to a prominence which, by the middle of the second century AD, produced a Presiding Elder. Very soon there was a Bishop of the Church with the rest of the elders known as 'presbyters'. Later a 'Bishopric' came to include many Churches under the jurisdiction of one Bishop. 'Apostolic Sees', 'Archbishoprics', 'Cardinals' and the like soon became features of a system of clerical hierarchy. The primacy of Rome was clearly accepted by the tenth century and the designation 'Pope' or 'Father' emerged for the Bishop of that city. In contradiction of the plain teaching of Scripture, a sharp distinction developed between the clergy and the laity, the clergy alone exercising the gifts of ministering to the people. This was a distortion of the clear teaching of the Lord and His apostles with regard to the rule and government of the Churches, and the Spirit-led exercise of varied gifts.

Total Declension

In these and in many other ways the clear and simple authority of the Word of God was undermined and disregarded. Papal authority, formalised centuries later in the doctrine of infallibility, came to command equal authority with Scripture and this was exploited by evil men who occupied high office in a corrupt Church of Rome. Darkness descended upon that which had in apostolic days such a bright and glorious prospect. For almost a thousand years, until the dawning of the Reformation, great fundamental truths were generally lost sight of.

It may be claimed that in recent years some denominations which retain episcopal hierarchy and infant sprinkling have tended to modify the emphasis they once placed on these. They now acknowledge to some extent the New Testament teaching of the priestly heritage of all believers, and of believers' baptism by immersion. This is good as far as it goes, but it will be sad if such awakenings only result in an uncomfortable accommodation between some Christians who have perceived the importance of long-neglected New Testament truths, and others who are content, or prefer, to stay with practices and teachings which effectively deny these. This may be a new dimension of the very dubious concept of the 'visible church' where believers and unconverted people are seen to be associated in the various denominations, each individual being regarded as responsible to God alone, for his or her 'membership' basis. Surely this cannot be seen as expressing the New Testament pattern of divine service in Churches of God, striving to represent truly God's Kingdom on earth. More will be said about some of these matters presently.

CHAPTER TWO: THE WAY BACK

———

AS THE CENTURIES SUCCEEDED one another further heresies and unscriptural practices were multiplied, especially in the Roman Catholic Church. The original simplicity and purity of the Faith had yielded to a vast system of false doctrine and practice. Instead of the two divine ordinances of Baptism and the Breaking of the Bread, there now are seven 'sacraments', including infant baptism, regarded as a necessary condition of salvation, and even 'extreme unction' as a terminal rite. The Breaking of the Bread had become a sacrifice in the form of the 'Mass'. Above all, the authority of the 'Church' and its papal head, had usurped the all-authority of the Master and His Word through His apostles. Rome ensured that the Bible was a closed book among the people generally.

A Lamp to My Feet

Yet in the midst of Rome's darkness, God ensured this one essential purpose for the future-the preservation of the necessary manuscripts and other documents for the Book which would again shed its divine light world-wide in happier days. An important contribution was Jerome's monumental fourth century work, in which he advocated acceptance of the Hebrew canon of the Old Testament, excluding certain apocryphal books. He translated most of the Bible into Latin and in the sixth century his work was incorporated into the Vulgate. This

Latin Version was used as the basis for early translations of the Scriptures into English. The English Bible has in its turn been extensively translated into many other languages to spread the light of God's truth across the world.

Down the ages there has, however, been a remarkable preservation of choice truths in relatively isolated areas. God never left Himself without witness. Men and women of great spiritual valour gave their lives in such places as Armenia. There was noble resistance to the Roman Catholic inquisition in the thirteenth century; the Waldensian movement also developed in Europe about this time and monks were crossing from Ireland to Scotland with a message certainly a great deal purer than anything Rome had to offer. Such were men and women whose hearts God had touched and who resolutely preserved, or recovered, many of the precious New Testament truths. But the renewed vision which ultimately led back to New Testament Churches of God had to await men with an open Bible in their hands, the climax of the thrilling history of the English Bible and of the Reformation heroes associated with its production.

Spiritual Heroes

God was preparing spiritual Davids to tackle the Goliath of Rome in the Name of the God of the Word. As the fifteenth century gave way to the sixteenth, God was bringing forth strong men of faith in Europe. Space allows only passing mention of Luther, Zwingli, Calvin and others; or of their noble British counterparts in Tyndale, Coverdale, Latimer, Knox and a host of dedicated kindred spirits. Then the Wesleys and Whitefield led us into relatively modern times. Still, it is sobering to remember that C.H. Spurgeon, who died in 1892, had devoted much of his latter years in the Baptist Church to combating a mounting threat to truly evangelical witness which had been so dearly bought. The evangelism of D.L. Moody and Ira D. Sankey also flourished about this time. The Y.M.C.A. movement was established and illustrious names including George Müller, Dr Barnardo, and William Booth of the Salvation Army grace the history of the second half of the nineteenth century.

Awakenings

We concentrate at this point on Christian development in Britain because the next important chapter of our story unfolds in the British Isles as the Spirit of God began to work in another and quite distinctive manner. Similar awakenings were, of course, taking place in other countries including America from where Moody came to Britain. Throughout the nineteenth century many godly men, including some of those named above, became increasingly concerned about the reproach to the Name of Christ of the many divisions amongst believers and about the errors associated with systems of clergy. They laid fresh emphasis on the paramount importance of the authority of the Scriptures, and the original ambitions and desires of the Lord Jesus and His apostles for "them also that believe on Me through their word" (John 17:20). Furthermore, there was a growing awareness of the importance given by the Lord to the Breaking of the Bread and His evident desire that all of His own should observe this precious ordinance in its original simplicity and beauty.

CHAPTER THREE: THE RETURN TO SIMPLICITY

———

THE BRETHREN MOVEMENT

This brings us to that part of our narrative which calls for rather more detailed treatment in tracing the fuller recovery of New Testament truth about Churches of God in our time. It is the development of what has come to be known as the Christian Brethren movement, and it was this movement which initially provided the rich soil from which grew the present testimony of Churches of God in the Fellowship of the Son of God. It prepared a foundation for the rebuilding of the House of God, yet not all the early doctrinal foundation stones then laid corresponded truly to the "foundation of the apostles and prophets" (Eph.2:20). Such is the conviction of those in Churches of God today. They salute many of the fine men of God who emerged in the Brethren movement; nevertheless they are convinced that the achievements and progress of that movement as a whole fell short of re-establishing the divine pattern of service of God's House. This made necessary the separation which later took place.

The beginnings of the Christian Brethren movement have been well and carefully chronicled by several writers, including Neatby, Veitch, Noel, and Coad. Not surprisingly, the writings of these men, though essentially historical, reflect some of their personal views on directions which the movement took at various points. In the main, however, they agree on the principal course of events.

Great Men of the Early Days

Men of very different conditions of life, of ecclesiastical standing or association, came together in the early years of the nineteenth century to share an exercise of the Holy Spirit in their hearts. Prominent among these pioneers were A.X. Groves, J.G. Bellett, J.N. Darby and Dr E. Cronin. Other distinguished names soon emerged including George Müller of Bristol, a man of immense faith; G.V. Wigram, the concordance compiler; S.P. Tregelles, a distinguished textual scholar; W. Kelly and C.H. Mackintosh, able expositors of the Scriptures. A prime mover was Edward Cronin who was born in Cork in 1801. He was a Roman Catholic and in due course he qualified in medicine. He was converted to Christ and became enlightened about the one-ness of the Church which is Christ's Body. Joined by Edward Wilson in 1825, they kept the Breaking of the Bread in Wilson's home in Dublin. Soon this first little gathering of 'brethren' increased in number to seven and in 1827 J.N. Darby and J.G. Bellett joined their company. By then they were meeting in a large room in Mr Francis Hutchinson's house at 9 Fitzwilliam Square. Dublin and in 1830 they rented their first hired meeting room in 11 Aungier Street, Dublin, the purpose of their gathering being to let the Lord's table become more of a witness. So began a movement which struck a chord in the hearts of many spiritually exercised people (1).

The Basis of the Movement

It is very important at this point to understand what these men and women of God perceived themselves as doing. They recognised serious errors in the Roman Catholic and Established Churches, and to a lesser extent in the non-conformist Churches such as Methodist and Baptist. However they were very much not in the business of establishing a new denomination in complete separation from these other bodies. Their primary concern was to express re-discovered truths concerning the Church which is Christ's Body, and the priestly heritage of all believers, notably as we have seen, in the keeping of the Breaking of the Bread on the Lord's day. This approach later changed, as we shall see.

The Ground of Gathering

In pursuing this primary aim they were at some pains, therefore, not to require or even encourage Christians who joined them to separate themselves in all spheres of service from the denomination to which they belonged. Rather they stressed the welcome awaiting all believers who wished to join them, particularly for the Breaking of the Bread. The basis of their gathering is summed up in words written by W B. Neatby as follows: "A circle was to be drawn just wide enough to include all the children of God, and to exclude all who did not come under that category" (2) and by C.H. Mackintosh: "We should so meet that all the members of Christ's Body might, simply as such, sit down with us and exercise whatever gifts the Head of the Church has bestowed upon them" (3). Mr Müller and Mr Craik in Bristol concluded: "We ought to receive all whom Christ has received, irrespective of the measure of grace or knowledge which they have attained unto" (4).

Because of the importance of this issue to the subsequent emergence of the Churches of God, it cannot be too strongly emphasised at this point that the basis of fellowship of the early brethren was the common life in Christ enjoyed by all believers. It was *not* any fuller confession of obedience to the Lord's will, or separation from error in other denominations, although the latter did come about in the cases of many individuals and some companies. A growing sense of much that was wrong in the existing denominations inevitably led many to feel unable to continue any association with them, but the basis of the gathering of brethren was common life in Christ or joint membership of the Church, the Body of Christ. This principle of gathering is further amplified in a quotation from A.N. Groves:

"I ever understood our principle of communion to be the possession of the common life ... of the family of God ... these were our early thoughts, and they are my most mature ones ... I naturally unite fixedly with those in whom I see and feel most of the life and power of God. But I am as free to visit other Churches where I see much disorder as to visit the houses of my friends, though they govern them not as I would wish" (5).

It is not the intention of this historical summary to make extensive quotations from historians and the early leaders of the Brethren movement. Our main purpose is to provide a brief historical review from which those who are interested can glean an insight into the origins of contemporary Churches of God and the fundamental reasons why a separation in testimony was felt to be necessary. An earlier publication of the Churches of God also entitled 'The Search for the Truth of God' makes more extensive use of quotations and this is invaluable for any who wish to study the subject in slightly greater depth. Though no longer in print, many copies still exist.

Thus we see the mind of early brethren with regard to the basis of gathering expressed quite clearly and explicitly. We must submit, at this stage of our historical journey, the crucial question; Was the basis of fellowship of the early brethren the same as that which the New Testament teaches for the Churches of God in Jerusalem, Antioch, Ephesus, Corinth and all the others? It is our firm conviction that it was not; and the subsequent history of the Brethren movement proves that this early basis of fellowship could not be sustained.

References: 1. Information derived from T.S. Veitch, *The Story of the Brethren Movement,* pp. 13-15. 2. *A History of the Plymouth Brethren,* W.B. Neatby. p. 28. 3. *Life and Times of Josiah*, C.H. Mackintosh, p. 50. 4. Quoted in T.S. Veitch, op.cit., p. 37. 5. Quoted in W.B. Neatby, op.cit., pp. 61-63.

CHAPTER FOUR:
CONTINUING THE BRETHREN
STORY

EXTENSION AND DEVELOPMENT

As the first half of the nineteenth century advanced, assemblies of Christian Brethren grew up all over the British Isles, in the continents of Europe and America, and in other parts of the world. Plymouth, England had early become the location of a growing company of Brethren, led by some able men, notably B.W. Newton; thus originating the often-used designation 'Plymouth Brethren'. There the worthy aspirations of the believers gathered together were to live in close fellowship with the Lord in holiness and love, walking worthily of Him and animating the hope of His return. Difficulties arose in Plymouth, however, when two of the leading men, B.W. Newton and J.L. Harris, who had become recognised as overseers, began ministering the Word on alternate Lord's Days.

This practice was acceptable to some, but others were unhappy with it because of the inevitable restrictions it imposed on the exercise of gift by other brethren. The situation in Plymouth had become complicated by the adoption by Mr Newton of certain teachings about the Person of the Lord Jesus which many of his fellows frankly felt were in error. The precise issue centred on the Lord's sufferings, Mr Newton teaching that the Lord Jesus came under divine wrath in contexts other than His vicarious sufferings on the cross. Mr Newton subsequently retracted this teaching. When J.N. Darby returned in 1845 from a very successful seven-year evangelical preaching tour in Switzerland, he was asked to go to Plymouth to give counsel and help. Perhaps because he strongly shared in the condemnation of Mr Newton's disputed teachings, Mr Darby did not effect reconciliation and, in October that year, he took the drastic step of leading some sixty people into gathering separately from the main body of Brethren in Plymouth. The resulting two companies in Plymouth then met quite separately from one another and apparently with no fellowship between them.

Problems in Bristol

Two men from the company with which Mr Newton was associated went to live in Bristol and asked for fellowship in Bethesda Chapel there, the local spiritual home of Mr Müller, of orphanage fame. After it had been determined that these two brothers did not share Mr Newton's views on the matter in doctrinal dispute about the Person of the Lord, they were received in Bristol. However, some there objected and withdrew from the Bethesda Chapel meeting. Mr Darby became involved, and after long discussions with Mr Müller in Bristol, he firmly dissociated himself from the Bethesda Chapel fellowship because of their reception of the two brothers from Plymouth.

It would appear that Mr Darby was not satisfied with the way in which the Bristol assembly had exonerated the two men from Plymouth with regard to Mr Newton's teachings. He pressed them to issue a clear and open condemnation of the teachings, but they felt this was not called for, although they subsequently did make a statement which effectively dissociated themselves from the erroneous teaching. Mr Darby vigorously pressed his views throughout many Brethren assemblies at this time on what came to be known as the 'Bethesda Question'. He ultimately issued a circular from Leeds in 1848 effectively cutting off not only Bethesda Chapel, but also all other assemblies who received anyone who went there. Those companies which followed Mr Darby soon came to be known as 'Exclusive' and those which refused to follow him, as 'Open'.

This is, of course, a highly condensed version of the events leading to the major split in the Brethren movement, an event which obviously had far-reaching effects and which is chronicled in greater detail in histories of the movement. It is from some of these, notably 'The Story of the Brethren Movement' by T.S. Veitch, and 'A History of the Plymouth Brethren' by W.B. Neatby, that the events referred to above have mainly been culled. The original vision of entirely free access to fellowship in the assemblies of all who truly belonged to Christ, expressed by Mr Darby as well as other early leaders, was by this time thoroughly changed, and indeed almost wholly out of sight. Such was certainly the case as far as the Exclusive assemblies were concerned, considering the very nature of their origins and the way in which the regulation of their affairs and the government of their assemblies developed.

The Changing Basis of Fellowship

Concerning the so-called Open companies, whose origins as such are generally linked to Bristol, it can be seen that their beginnings were involved in the decision of Mr Müller and his fellow leaders to receive the two men from Plymouth. Why, we might ask, should there have been any question, from their point of view, since the two men were undoubtedly true believers and fellow-members of the Church, the Body of Christ? Is it not apparent that we have here the beginnings of a form of words which, with slight variations, has since been frequently employed by believers in Open assemblies to indicate the grounds on which Christians may be received to their fellowship-words such as 'all those who are sound in faith and godly in life'? (It seems clear that a judgement was made at Bristol that the two brothers from Plymouth met such criteria).

It is apparent that such a formula has an entirely different basis from the simple primary principle of the first assemblies 'common life in Christ'. The use of such words as 'sound in faith and godly in life' illustrate the inadequacy of this principle as providing a sound basis for the fellowship and gathering of Christians. Yet today, among those groups of Christians which no longer wish to be seen as too selective in regard to those they receive, the 'open table' continues to be widely practised.

While these departures from the originally stated basis were taking place there is no indication that the leaders of the various factions in the Brethren movement ever tried to reach a consensus by collectively reverting to the New Testament pattern of unity, although this was surely the appropriate thing to do.

In tracing how God led believers back from the darkness which engulfed Christendom in the Middle Ages to a new age of spiritual enlightenment, the Brethren movement was, we believe, a very important stage in this noble journey. However, on this matter of the basis of gathering we believe that what might have been a fuller witness to the truth of God in our day became progressively weakened by disagreements until today, when it is sadly acknowledged by many in the movement that the original mould of the Brethren assemblies has been broken.

Pursuing the Road Back

It may seem presumptuous to some other Christians that the Churches of God in the Fellowship of the Son of God today should claim to have been able to complete the journey when the main stream of 'Brethrenism' went astray on the important matter of the basis of gathering. The Churches of God, we believe by divine guidance, returned to clear New Testament principles for Christians functioning together in worship and witness.

We shall now try to explain some of the issues which were vital to the understanding of those who separated from their former association among the Brethren assemblies to form the present fellowship of assemblies, the Churches of God. In so doing we wish to recognise and pay tribute to the personal godliness and devotion to the Person of our Lord Jesus Christ of many of the brethren who chose not to separate. Sadly, it has been the case that some of the loveliest and most fragrant Christian lives have been lived out in service with associations and denominations whose scriptural basis and teachings cannot measure up to the Word of God as we understand it. In His wisdom and grace our God will surely richly reward such personal piety. Such godliness presents a strong challenge to Christians who feel led of God to contend earnestly for important truths. Their own spiritual condition needs to be examined and re-examined before the Lord to maintain a balance between doctrinal or positional rectitude and personal life and testimony.

The Use of the Term 'Church'

It is important for us at this point to examine the way in which the word 'Church' was used in the early days of the Brethren. The histories of this period show that expressions such as 'the Church of God on earth' and 'the Church of Christ' were used rather loosely without recognition that they are not terms used in the Scriptures, and are indeed terms which lack clear definition when they are used. In using the term 'the Church of God on earth' many doubtless understood it to embrace all the members of the Church the Body of Christ alive on earth at any one time, while others may have seen it as describing all those gathered visibly in some kind of collective witness and service. If the latter definition was in mind, what associations and denominations would be included and which excluded?

Surely it is immediately and compellingly relevant that the New Testament speaks of 'the Church of God' and 'Churches of God', of 'the Church which is His Body, once of 'the Churches of Christ', though never of 'the Church of Christ'. How can we expect clearly to expound the Word of God regarding church truths or issues of rule and government when there is confusion in the use of such terms as 'Church' and 'Churches'? We firmly submit the answer must be that we cannot. The early Brethren should have considered more closely the use made of these terms by the Holy Spirit in the Scriptures and the connections in which they are used. This should have saved them and those who followed them much sorrow and division in the history of the movement.

CHAPTER FIVE:
CONSTITUTIONAL ISSUES

———

IN THE VERY EARLY DAYS of the Brethren, believers from any denomination could come together to break bread and subsequently, even on the same Lord's day, return to activities in their own church group. The question soon had to be faced as to whether the 'Brethren' companies should themselves have a constitution as Churches. Many saw the inconsistency of making what was in effect a witness against the error of the denominations, with their neglect of many scriptural principles, and at the same time continuing to support and have fellowship with them. It is a great pity that a resolute re-examination of the first principles as outlined in the New Testament did not take place at this time.

A Scriptural Constitution

The Churches of God today are sometimes criticised for making Acts 2:41,42 a proof text for their constitution and practice, though in greater or lesser degree many Open assemblies would claim to follow its basic tenets. These verses directly tell us how the first Church of God in Jerusalem was established. Those who had believed were baptised as disciples of the Lord Jesus Christ. Then there was *addition,* not surely any kind of casual reception to fellowship for the day, month or whatever, but a clear, permanent, public reception by the Church. For they then *continued* in the four key spiritual disciplines and exercises, namely, the apostles' doctrine, the fellowship, the Breaking of the Bread, and the prayers. These bound the early disciples into a secure, well-definedand identifiable company of witnessing Christians who formed the Church of God in Jerusalem.

Of course, the problem did not then exist of some believers belonging to another Christian Church or group, but that does not really affect the issue. Adherence to this divinely established example and pattern for all the Churches in unity would, we submit, have kept the early Brethren movement on course. As it was, we find a record in Mr Veitch's 'Story of the Brethren Movement' (pp.40-41) of a letter received by Mr Müller of Bristol from believers in Germany, enquiring about the principles held and practised by the Bristol assembly. Mr Müller responded with a visit to Stuttgart from where the enquiry had come. At first there was much happy fellowship and much in common with the Christians there who seemed to meet on similar lines to the Bristol meeting, until it emerged that his 'open' attitude to communion permitted the reception of unbaptised believers. At this point some of the devout Baptist Christians who shared in the fellowship of the group at Stuttgart protested that baptism should be insisted upon. Others took exception to sharing the Breaking of the Bread with those from the state Church whose systems of clergy they felt to be unscriptural.

It is a little difficult to understand how men of the standing of Mr Müller and his contemporaries did not see that problems of this kind were inevitable, and that discussion together, with submission to one another in the light of Scripture, could have resolved them and preserved the unity of the assemblies.

The Problems of Strong Individual Leaders

Following the division referred to earlier which resulted in Exclusive and Open companies of Brethren, the assemblies on both sides of the divide had no settled mode of government, were independent of one another and had no agreed provision for the resolution of difficulties which might occur. Although the errors of a system of clergy had been appreciated by many of the early Brethren, the dangers of the emergence of dominant individual leaders among them seem to have been less readily perceived.

It has already been noted that progressive division among the initial Brethren groups originated in the separation into two companies in Plymouth, one led by Mr Newton and the other by Mr Darby. Then the problem spread to Bristol and very soon Mr Darby issued his circular letter from Leeds in 1848, in effect excommunicating all assemblies of Brethren which were not willing to share his repudiation of the Bristol Bethesda action in receiving the two brothers from Plymouth. The decision to receive them seems to have been based on a suspension of judgement on the issue of doctrinal error which was allegedly being taught by Mr Newton in Plymouth. Mr Darby could not tolerate what he regarded as an irresolute attitude towards the teaching of seriously wrong doctrine. In fact, however, we are surely driven to conclude, on the evidence of the history of those days, that, despite the faults of others concerned, the personal attitude of Mr Darby was central to the dispute and consequent division among the assemblies. He presumed to take an initiative which should never lie with any individual, except perhaps an apostle in New Testament times.

The Principles of Elderhood Disregarded

There is a clear scriptural pattern in the New Testament to guide disciples of our Lord Jesus Christ in this very important matter of leadership and church government, and it is a fundamental issue concerning the existence and the constitution of the Churches of God today. The New Testament writings point to individual Churches with elders who are responsible to the Lord, firstly for the local Church, then jointly for maintaining the unity of doctrine and practice in all the Churches. There is. we confidently submit, evidence that the Churches of God in New Testament times were linked together administratively for matters of common interest and concern by a united elderhood.

The unity of the Spirit which should be seen throughout the assemblies is, we believe, given expression to by an elderhood whose joint and collective responsibility embraces all the Churches of God. We believe that this issue of a united elderhood lay at the root of the division and fragmentation of the developing Brethren movement. For whatever reason, the leaders of the day set aside the guidance in the Word of God as to how assemblies united in testimony should be served by elders and an elderhood. In all justice and with respect to two great men of Bristol, Mr Müller and Mr Craik, it must be recorded that they had given very serious and prayerful consideration to the issue of leadership and elders in the local assembly. They concluded that the mind of the Lord was for the recognition of elders in each company who would give guidance to the assembly on matters of doctrine and, where necessary, discipline. The latter would, however, be reserved, and correctly so, for final settlement in the presence of the Church.

The Example of Acts 15

There was no wider application of this principle, however, nor does it appear that serious consideration had been given to the example of Acts 15. There it is evident that men of apostolic standing in that day introduced wider elderhood counsel and, under the Holy Spirit's guidance, were able collectively to issue decrees on the subjects in question for all the Churches (Acts 16:4,5). The history of the Brethren movement might have been so very different had the leaders of that day been more prepared to seek for wider counsel among the other elders throughout the assemblies. The Jerusalem conference of apostles and elders is so fully recorded in Acts 15 that it must surely be regarded as an example for the elders among the people of God. It is the God-given way of striving towards unity of doctrine and practice among the Churches, and it is difficult to understand how it can be set aside if such unity is to be maintained. For a fuller treatment of this subject we refer readers to a parallel publication by Hayes Press, 'Elders and the Elderhood'.

The Church 'In Ruins'

The view that the Church is 'in ruins' is one which came to be widely embraced by many, mainly in the Exclusive sector. The claim would seem to have been that, in the face of all the divisions and differences among disciples today, it is impossible for the New Testament pattern of Christian witness and service to be realised. It is important to recognise that the acceptance of such a position appears to release brethren from any obligation to seek out and follow closely the divine and. scriptural pattern applying to the Churches of God of the New Testament. Such an attitude is, however, based on a false premise which centres on the meaning and use attributed to the term 'Church' in Mr Darby's central doctrine of the ruin of the Church. It is very difficult to understand what was meant exactly by 'the church' here. Perhaps it relates to further words of Mr Darby when he wrote: "The church on earth at each successive period, is thus the aggregate of the elect who are then manifested" (1).

Although the meaning of 'manifested' is also not wholly clear, we can only conclude that it refers to all true believers alive on earth at any one time or perhaps all identifiable by the quality of their Christian life and service. This, it must again be asserted, is not a scriptural use of the term 'Church': If, however, the term `the Church' were applied to all believers alive on earth, how could such be said to be 'in ruins'? The members of the Body of Christ as portrayed in such Scriptures as 1 Corinthians 12 and Ephesians 4, far from presenting a picture of 'ruin', are seen in vibrant harmony and expressing the lovely characteristics of their glorious Head. Scripture does not describe those members of the Body alive on earth at any one time in any collective terms which are different from those describing the whole.

If anything is in ruins, surely it can only be the House of God, identified quite distinctly from the Church the Body of Christ, identified indeed as a divinely ordained structure comprising the Churches of God in the New Testament. It was the clear desire and expectation of the Lord that all of His own, members indeed of His Body, should have part in the spiritual House or Temple. However, the reality is that New Testament history and teaching show that not all living members of the Body were in the House and Temple of God. The single sad matter of the apostolic instruction in 1 Corinthians 5:13 that the man ensnared in moral sin should be put away from the Church of God in Corinth, demonstrates this point.

Uses of the word ` Church' in the New Testament

The following uses of the word 'Church' are found in the New Testament but not one of them corresponds to what appears to have been Mr Darby's idea of the Church:

1.The secular use of the word Church, or assembly (Acts 19:32,39,41).

2.Israel, the Church in the wilderness (Acts 7:38).

3.The Church which is His (Christ's) Body (Matt.16:18; Eph.1.22,23, 5:27).

4.The Church of God and the Churches of God (1 Cor.1:2, 10:32, 11:16,22; 1 Thess.2:14; 2 Thess.1:4).

5.The Church of the Living God, the House of God (1 Tim.3:15; Heb.3:6, 10:21; 1 Pet.2:5, 4:17).

6.The Churches of Christ, the Churches of the saints, Churches at the house of... (Rom.16:5,16;1 Cor.14:33).

7.The Church of the firstborn (ones) (Heb.12:23).

Mr Darby's understanding of the word 'Church' seems to be an idea of his own and it cannot be aligned with the teaching of the apostles. It is the loose and unscriptural use of the word 'Church' that has led to much of the confusion of thought on ecclesiastical matters in some of the writings of the Brethren.

Supremacy of One Assembly Over Others

The Exclusive companies of Brethren had long since departed from the simple basis for fellowship which had been stated in the early days of the movement, and in 1875 Mr Darby wrote that: "... the assembly has to be satisfied as to the persons ... At the beginning it was not so, i.e. there was no such examination. Now I believe it a duty according to 2 Tim.2:2" (2).

The important point we wish to register here is once again the reality that 'common life' in Christ could not, and should not, be made the sole basis of assembly fellowship. Indeed for many years believers seeking fellowship in an Exclusive assembly had to give assurance of 'having judged the question'; that is, the question which had divided Müller and Darby in the early days of Bristol. This illustrates Mr Darby's authoritative personal attitude. To maintain doctrinal soundness and uniformity of practice throughout the Exclusive assemblies Mr Darby adopted an approach which was grievously flawed. For the assemblies were required to acknowledge the authority of the Park Street company in London in regard to matters of doctrine and administration. This practice, followed for many years, had no foundation in Scripture. Not even the first Church of God in Jerusalem occupied that role in New Testament times. We re-affirm with assurance that there was available to them a biblical pattern, precedent, and example of how Churches should be constituted and governed, which they consistently disregarded.

The Position of Open Assemblies

By contrast to the Exclusive companies, the Open companies pursued a variety of courses, differing from assembly to assembly, on this important matter of the basis of gathering. They also differed widely in the degree of fellowship they had with other denominations, and indeed also with other companies of Brethren. While some sought to maintain the original approach of receiving all believers to their fellowship, and in particular to the Lord's table for the Breaking of the Bread, others unmistakably moved their position. This has resulted in a large proportion of Open companies receiving all who are (a) born again; (b) sound in faith; and (c) godly in life. These would appear to be very satisfactory parameters to apply so long as there is clear understanding about the interpretation of 'sound in faith' in particular.

It may be claimed that being sound in faith applies to a range of issues of fundamental Christian doctrine such as the foundation truths about the Person and work of the Lord Jesus Christ and the inerrancy of Holy Scripture. So far as it goes that is excellent, but should it not also extend to other matters which are commanded by the Lord but which some have labelled 'non-essentials'? The outstanding example is that of believers' baptism. The fact that Open assemblies vary in their attitude here, illustrates the nature of the problem of the interpretation of 'sound in faith'. In the Churches of God we have always strongly believed that there is a distinct significance in the expression in Jude v.3: "the faith which was once for all delivered unto the saints."

The Faith

What then is 'the faith'? Evidently it has wider scope than 'our common salvation', for Jude was initially exercised to write to the saints about our common salvation but was guided by the Holy Spirit to write to exhort them to "contend earnestly for the faith which was once for all delivered unto the saints". Surely it must refer to a body of doctrine which calls for earnest diligence if its integrity and expression are to be maintained.

Paul, when he speaks to the elders of Ephesus (Acts 20:27), declares that he shrank not from declaring to them "the whole counsel of God". Paul was not a man for shrinking, yet it would seem that the witness of a full and rounded body of teaching called for a real effort of resolution on his part, perhaps in the face of a tendency by some to set aside some important doctrines on which saints were inclined to differ. To Timothy, Paul wrote "Hold the pattern of sound words" (2 Tim.1:13) and the epistles to Timothy contain careful instruction on elders and their work in maintaining that pattern.

Surely it cannot be within the New Testament pattern of sound words, for Christians in a company of believers which envisages its service as in line with the Churches of God in the New Testament, to move in and out of sectarian movements and denominations in their Christian service. And should such a company receive other believers to occasional fellowship in an assembly? Was the baptising and adding, and the continuing, of Acts 2.41,42 in some way optional or to be disregarded at will as a matter of convenience and freedom of fellowship? We must reply, surely not.

These points are made, not by way of disparagement, but of constructive criticism. As we proceed to examine the way in which Churches of God, united in testimony, came again into existence, striving for the New Testament pattern, the vastly important matter of the elderhood and its unity features prominently. The Open meetings have consistently maintained a position of full independence for each assembly and avoided any movement towards a united elderhood; practices which we believe with conviction to be divergent from the New Testament pattern.

References:1. Quoted in a *History of the Plymouth Brethren*, W.B. Neatby, p. 88. 2. Quoted in W.B. Neatby, op.cit., p. 218.

CHAPTER SIX: TO SEPARATE
OR NOT TO SEPARATE

———

TOWARDS THE END OF the nineteenth century the major issues touched on above came to weigh very heavily on the hearts of many who were at that time in the Open assemblies. Principal among these issues were the matters of the basis on which assemblies of saints should be gathered; the independence or inter-dependence of assemblies; and, closely linked to the latter, the whole pattern of rule and government through elders (overseers) such as were appointed in the New Testament Churches of God. Inextricably linked to these subjects were the questions concerning the meaning and expression of the House of God and the Kingdom of God.

The consideration of these practical issues and the awareness that they were not likely to become generally accepted by brethren, soon raised the highly sensitive matter of separation. Such separation would be primarily *to* the scriptural pattern contained in the Word of God, indeed to a full expression of 'the faith which was once for all delivered unto the saints'. Secondarily and reluctantly, yet as a matter of great importance, it would be separation *from* the associations and denominations which failed to give effect to the foundational truths of collective service. Some denominations had, indeed, as we have seen, gone so far historically as to reject the possibility of recovery of New Testament church truth and continued to take this position.

Growing Conviction to Separate

By the year 1876 some brothers and sisters in companies of Open Brethren felt a growing conviction that the Lord was calling them to move. There are two very important characteristics which stand out in these early moves which ultimately led to the establishment of the Churches of God as we know them today in the Fellowship of the Son of God, the Lord Jesus Christ.

The *first* was the widespread and spontaneous nature of the movement, mainly in the British Isles initially. This was not an exercise of heart of one or two who subsequently spread their teaching, and influenced others to follow, such as largely characterised the beginnings of the Exclusive movement in which Mr Darby played such a dominant personal role. The *second* encouraging feature of the movement we are now describing was the manifest reluctance to separate on the part of those who were, in the event, the prime movers. Their letters and the records of the meetings they called show how deeply they felt the pain of separation from fellow-believers with many of whom they had long served the Lord happily and in sweet fellowship. This was no cavalier, impetuous or self-promoting action as the contemporary correspondence bears out.

Questions in 'The Northern Witness'

In April 1876 certain questions were posed in 'The Northern Witness', a magazine which circulated widely among Christian Brethren assemblies. The questions were asked by Mr J.A. Boswell, and to them he offered his own answers in subsequent numbers of the magazine. A few years later in 1883 - for this development took years of patient discussion and searching of heart to mature - a pamphlet appeared entitled 'The Church and Churches of God', by Mr F.A. Banks. It offered a very concise and systematic statement of church truth which the author believed was becoming clear to him and to others from the New Testament Scriptures. This pamphlet made quite an impact and proved a source of much help to many in clarifying some of the truths concerned. Over several years which followed, exercised brethren continued faithfully to set forth among their fellows, in oral and written ministry, their growing convictions about the New Testament truths of the House of God as expressed in Churches of God linked together in testimony and service. It was a new unfolding, we believe, through the Holy Spirit, of old truth from New Testament times and it may be useful at this point to summarise again the main Issues:

1. That the Church of God in any one town was one Church regardless of how many companies might compose it.

2. That only baptised and added believers should be received into the Churches of God and share in the Breaking of the Bread. Addition to one Church of God means addition to all.

3. That overseers should be recognised in each Church and, in addition, should act together in matters affecting all the Churches to maintain a unity of practice and doctrine.

4. That the Churches were inter-dependent on one another and not independent.

5. That the House of God was composed of all the Churches of God seen together, united in service.

The 'Needed Truth' Magazine for Promoting Church Truth

The Churches of God in fellowship today throughout the world have become generally identified with the magazine 'Needed Truth', so much so that they have sometimes been referred to as the 'Needed Truth movement'. This may be inevitable, if unfortunate, when a rather distinctively titled publication is associated uniquely with a particular line of teaching, for this is what happened from the first number of the magazine in 1888.

It was published quarterly until 1891 and was then a monthly periodical until 2008, when it reverted a to quarterly format. A group of editors has, since early days, been responsible to the Conference of Overseers of the Churches of God, representing the entire elderhood, for producing a magazine which kept clearly in view the unique purposes for which it originated; and at the same time aimed to present a comprehensive picture of biblical truth touching all the great doctrines of the faith. It also seeks to offer spiritual food of a devotional character and by the help of the divine Spirit, rightly to divide the Word of truth.

The magazine was, however, but a reflection of a spiritual exercise in the hearts of many in numerous assemblies of the Brethren. It was the organ of expression of deeply felt convictions which were also expressed in much correspondence and conferring together. A considerable quantity of the writings and letters of those days remains extant and could profitably be quoted in the course of this narrative. In the interest of reasonable brevity and readability, however, these have been kept to a minimum, though collected letters are readily available through the publisher of this booklet, to those who would like to study them further.

The Windermere Conference of 1891

A notable conference was called in 1891 by some of the brethren who had played a leading role in opening up the debate on church truth. It was held at Windermere, England, and was addressed by brethren who reflected different shades of opinion on the truths under examination. It is worth pausing to note one part of the debate which points to a typical issue of concern to many present and illustrates the sort of thing which led many to despair of seeing truly scriptural practices prevail among Open Brethren gatherings in general. The question was posed to one of the brethren who wished to adhere to existing 'Open' practices:

"Would you allow a Christian to break bread with you who presented himself at your assembly, but who did not wish to be received in fellowship?" The answer given was "Yes". A further question was then asked. "If you had an application from a Christian for reception to fellowship, would you keep the applicant sitting behind those in fellowship for one Lord's Day, until his testimony had been received by the assembly?" Again the answer was "Yes".

Now it may seem to some a relatively small matter just exactly how such situations were handled in practice, but it was believed then and is now, that such a situation displays an inconsistency calling for a thorough examination and application of New

Testament principles of church fellowship if effect is to be given to the Lord's will in these matters. We respectfully draw attention to other similar inconsistencies which have prevailed among Open Brethren from the beginning. Thus, individuals from two assemblies which do not share fellowship may find themselves worshipping together in a third assembly, often in a different town. This third assembly has felt free to receive both of them, yet they revert to their separate and separated assemblies on their return home. That such a situation indicates something deeply wrong and unscriptural, is surely obvious.

Growing Unease

The Windermere conference was inconclusive of any general decision or consensus among those present but it became evident to many concerned individuals and companies of Brethren that a point of decision was approaching. As a result, in the immediately succeeding years, mainly between 1892 and 1894, numerous letters were written setting out the reasons why groups of individuals, or in some instances all the saints in entire companies, felt they could no longer continue in association with assemblies of Open Brethren. They clearly heard the Lord calling them and others out, and into a scriptural position and unity of testimony which they firmly believed expressed the constitution and pattern of New Testament Churches of God forming an earthly habitation of God in the Spirit (Eph.2:22). It was then, and is now, very much a matter of positively seeking in appropriate humility, without which the movement would be justly suspect, to obey 'that form of teaching whereunto ye were delivered' (Rom.6:17) and the 'pattern of sound words' (2 Tim.1:13). It was in no sense an attempt to disparage others who were active in Christian witness and service in whatever denomination they were found. We can be assured that the Lord will evaluate and reward their service with unerring wisdom.

A Time for Decision

From such places as Cardiff and Cromer, Liverpool and London, Belfast and Glasgow and from many other gatherings came brief but positive statements in all of which real exercise of heart was evident, together with a clear appeal to Scripture. The leading of God's Spirit was clearly felt and, while some letters appeared as early as 1892, others followed more than two years later as the result of waiting upon God and 'waiting one for another'. One example was a letter dated December 1892 from which we quote:

"We the undersigned, after long and patient waiting in hope of a better state of things being brought about in the assemblies in and around ... believe in ourselves that the time has come when, at the bidding of the Lord, we must come out from that so-called fellowship in which we have been. It is with much sorrow of heart we take this step, for we may have to leave many behind whom we love in the Lord ... There are those who receive with open arms those who at the bidding of the Lord have been put away from another assembly; also receiving those who have gone away in open rebellion. By doing so they put an end to all godly discipline ... Others will not allow a word to be said about separation or believers' baptism. Much more might be said, but we refrain as we believe that what we have said will be quite apparent to spiritually minded men who have eyes to see and ears to hear. Should the overseeing men of any assembly desire to have a conversation with us on this matter we shall be only too glad to meet with such."

Many such letters are on record.

How Long to Wait?

It is inevitable that, in the context of a historical survey, the question will recur, Should not those brethren and sisters who were exercised about church truth and the House of God have waited longer and tried to influence their fellows, rather than separate themselves? The answer to that question can only be found in a wider perusal of the letters which were written at the time. They show very clearly that there was an unmistakable rejection by the majority within the Open meetings of the convictions which were growing among a minority. The decisions to move came only after much pleading and heart-searching.

Of course, there were also many who shared in considerable measure the persuasion of those who separated, but for whom the cost was too high. That cost for many involved relinquishing old friendships forged in active service together over many years, and some even had to face strains and some distancing within their families. In such instances, of course, the cost of separation was felt also by those who did not come out. Let it be noted, however, that it is believed among the Churches of God, that family relationships are very important and precious in God's sight and that differences in beliefs and in resultant locations of Christian service, should occasion only the minimum disturbance in the family circle. Unnecessarily severe disruption in the family circle has brought disrepute on some Exclusive companies in recent years.

Coming Out

It is generally understood in the Churches of God that by about 1894 the present testimony had been gathered into one. Inevitably there cannot be precision about this since it was over a period of years that the elders of the separated companies came to recognise clearly the true extent of their numbers and distribution. In September 1894 at a conference of elders of the Churches of God it was agreed to publish a list of assemblies by Districts. Certainly such a list, dating from 1898 is extant with reference to Scotland, and by 1906 a more comprehensive list of Churches of God had been produced and circulated.

It has always been a strong conviction in the Churches of God that a united elderhood was crucial to the establishment and preservation of divinely ordered unity among a scripturally gathered people. Therefore from the earliest years there have been regular international conferences of representative elders from the different Districts of Churches of God. These have endeavoured, in subjection to the Holy Spirit's guidance, and to one another, to resolve issues of doctrine and practice for the guidance of all the Churches, and all on the basic pattern of Acts 15 and its striking example of godly unity.

A small group of elders, usually referred to as 'leading brethren', is entrusted by the conference of elders with giving counsel and, where necessary, advising on interim action which may be necessary between Conferences. They also make the arrangements for the elders' Conferences and prepare the agenda, mainly from items submitted by Districts. All the activities and actions of these brethren are submitted to Conference for confirmation and comment. In no sense do they form part of any elderhood hierarchy.

Is There a Real Difference?

The question might be asked, 'Is there any real difference between the character and conduct of the Churches of God which separated and the companies of Open Brethren which were left'? Since the beginning of the Brethren movement there have been marked differences between individual companies of Open Brethren, some having been more 'open' than others. (It is realised that today some gatherings previously known as Brethren assemblies are preferring to adopt other titles such as 'Brethren Church' or 'Evangelical Church'.) However, some of these companies still welcome to the Lord's table anyone professing faith in Christ; others insist on baptism for fellowship, and some apply an even more extensive test of 'sound in faith' and 'godly in life'.

There are certain groupings among some of these companies in that they recognise each other in a common affinity of understanding of doctrine and practice, and share links such as lists of assemblies and letters of commendation. Nevertheless they all stand firm on the issue of the essential independence of each assembly in all matters of the regulation of their teaching and practice. They do not recognise a need for a common elderhood forum such as is mentioned above in respect of Churches of God. This we believe to be scripturally necessary if true unity is to be preserved.

It is not surprising therefore that those in Churches of God should sometimes be challenged by Christian friends in other assemblies as to the essential difference between the two. This is particularly likely where such an assembly has very strict and rigorous criteria for admission to fellowship; and in most of its practices, including the local operation of overseers or elders, differs hardly at all from a Church of God in the movement we are now reviewing.

In fact in the final analysis an essential difference does exist in that each Church of God in fellowship is linked definitely and perceptibly with other Churches through the unity of the elderhood and, notwithstanding acknowledged human imperfection and failure, all are subject to one another in the fear of Christ. A movement which stands together with links as strong as that exemplified in Acts 16:4,5 will always be distinguished from others, however similar in local church practice they may appear: "And as they went on their way ... they delivered them the decrees for to keep, which had been ordained of the apostles and elders that were at Jerusalem. So the churches were strengthened in the faith, and increased in number daily." It is the conviction of the Churches of God today that a contemporary expression of House of God truth requires no less than this distinction and identification.

An Occasion of Failure

It was a failure in this matter of the functioning of the united elderhood in the early formative years which led in 1901 to the separation of a number of assemblies in Scotland from the re-established Churches of God. Generally known as the 'Vernal trouble', the problem centred on action in a matter of church discipline in one of the Churches by certain overseers. They were unwilling to wait long enough or consult widely enough, to achieve a unity of mind about the action they considered necessary. The whole sad event led to a reaffirming of the commitment of the Churches of God to unity in decisions and actions among elders and in the Churches also.

Doctrine and Practice

While we lay great stress upon positional teaching we are not unaware of the importance of maintaining a balance so that position is matched by a corresponding condition. The Churches of God today realise that the positional stand they take on House of God truth makes great demands in terms of this essential godly balance in spiritual service and Christian life generally. We recognise an admirable sanctification in terms of personal holiness and Christian service in many fellow-believers from whom we are sadly separated in service, and this challenges our hearts deeply. To maintain a scriptural blend of position and condition calls for confession and supplication for oft-renewed grace. At the same time our conviction holds firm on the doctrine of "the faith which was once for all delivered unto the saints".

CHAPTER SEVEN: IS SEPARATION STILL NECESSARY?

THIS REVIEW OF EVENTS leading up to the separation which took place between 1892 and 1894 seeks to explain the reasons why it occurred. However, a century and a quarter has elapsed since then and some, particularly younger disciples in Churches of God, may wonder if the separated position which the Churches maintain continues to be justified. Does the doctrinal error and the disorder in church government and practice still exist which would justify our separation? It gives us no satisfaction to claim that the reasons do still exist, and in fact have intensified, particularly in recent decades.

Confusion About Unity

As we observe the Christian world an increasing confusion over doctrinal matters is evident. Fundamental Christian beliefs are being challenged and often denied. While at one time such challenges mainly originated with the liberal theologians, they are now also coming from the evangelical sector of Christendom. In Britain the British Council of Churches, which has tried since 1942 to link denominations on a very 'broad church' basis, has ceased to exist. In its place has emerged a new 'Inter-church Process' or 'Churches Together' with distinct, though linked, ecumenical organisations for various parts of the UK. This new movement has, significantly, secured the active involvement of the Roman Catholic Church as well as the major national and non-conformist Churches such as Baptist and Methodist. Much of the 'charismatic' movement is also in sympathy.

As a result, many devout evangelical Christians are expressing great alarm and are setting up alternative 'unity' organisations. Such are, however, based solely on a unity of faith in the basic truths of the gospel, resulting in an informal association of Churches without true unity and fellowship in doctrine and practice. There is no attempt to express the comprehensive New Testament pattern of discipleship and church truth as presented in this booklet. Similar developments are taking place in other countries.

The Christian Brethren movement itself, which began with such promise, is now being disrupted by such issues as the so-called 'charismatic' gifts and the place and role of women in the assemblies. The movement's original identity has been largely lost and the name Christian Brethren may soon cease to be used or recognised.

Relationships with Other Christians

It is wonderfully true that there is an immediate bond between all children of God who by word or action reveal their faith and love towards our Lord Jesus Christ. "How blessed is the tie that binds believers' hearts in one." The witness that this can give to the world is priceless. Yet sadly, is it not true that personal friendships and fellowship between Christians can be overshadowed by the confused denominational picture we see of these same Christians at worship and in service to God? Christian colleagues who stand shoulder to shoulder in witness for Christ in the workplace may find that they differ in the very primary matter of baptism. In this way, that which might have been a fruitful and productive joint witness is impaired when one neglects the clear command of the Lord to be baptised; and so the Christian unity which they may wish to strive for is unattainable in the absence of a common obedience to the Word of God.

The Bible's Answer on Unity

In a deeply sincere and genuine effort to overcome such evident problems some Christian teachers counsel those young in faith to join themselves to a 'Bible-believing Church'; or, to associate with Christians 'sound in life and faith'. True, it is no bad starting point to eliminate as mentors any who have less than total commitment to the inerrancy of Holy Scripture. Such advice cannot be faulted - as far as it goes. But it inevitably begs the question as to how the said Church applies and expresses its trust in the Word of God; or what are the criteria of 'soundness' in Christian doctrine. So we return to the deep significance of such New Testament expressions as "obedient from the heart to that form of teaching whereunto ye were delivered" (Rom.6:17).

Can we really expect that the Holy Spirit would instruct men at the beginning of this age in the establishment of a people for God and a holy nation, without the provision in Scripture for all time of a body of doctrine which would be an enduring foundation for a united testimony and service? If the answer is 'No', then surely we must conclude that such a body of teaching, such a pattern of divine service, exists in the Word; and that it is our solemn responsibility to search it out and to follow it without deviation. Can scriptural principles be observed and given expression to without a stand in separation from a confusing array of denominational Christian groups and 'Churches'? Is not the witness to these truths compromised if there is no separation from what is opposed to it?

Participation in Inter-denominational Activities

There has been increasing interest shown by Christian people in inter-denominational activity, especially in gospel outreach. Evangelically-minded believers from different denominations have co-operated for certain objectives such as overseas missionary work and large-scale gospel campaigns. Throughout their history over the past hundred and twenty-five years, the Churches of God have weighed very carefully the issues involved. They have done this firstly in the light of positive scriptural teaching on collective Christian service; and then, in consequence, in the light of the history described in this book of the re-emergence in our day of Churches of God according to the New Testament pattern. This development required progressive separation, firstly from the national Church and other major denominations (e.g. Baptist); and later from a Brethren movement which we believe failed to follow through its early promise of fuller recovery of New Testament church truth.

Reviewing the historical steps again, particularly from the point of view of Christian unity as perceived in inter-denominational work, we must re-emphasise the single scriptural pathway of service which was revealed, we believe, by the Holy Spirit for all believers of this dispensation. We have seen that, in the New Testament record, all the Churches of God were united in their common obedience to the one Lord, so bringing believers together at that time on a divinely ordained basis of united witness and service. There is no scriptural support for an association of believers on other grounds such as a temporary amalgamation for a limited objective.

The Answer of the Apostles

Preachers in apostolic times did not shrink from the consequences of preaching all that the Lord had commanded them (Acts 20:20,27). The basic principle of inter-denominationalism stands in pronounced contrast to the comprehensive witness of apostolic times to the 'apostles' doctrine', which itself found its foundation in the Great Commission of Matthew 28:18-20 - make disciples; baptise them; teach them to observe *all things* "whatsoever I commanded you". When we have been privileged to know the Lord's leading into a scriptural position we must have special regard for the truth of God which has been entrusted to us. To agree to differ on plainly revealed truths; to limit our testimony to but one aspect of the Lord's commission; to associate in witness with many whose doctrinal position we believe to be unscriptural; these are compromising expedients which cannot, we believe, stand the test of scriptural principle.

Wider Horizons for Disciples

Of course, the Lord blesses the gospel witness and devoted service of all who love and seek to follow Christ; and by whatever channel the saving message goes out the Lord, in His sovereign purpose of grace, builds precious members into that glorious purpose of our dispensation, the Church which is the Body of Christ. Yet the salvation of souls, however great the importance of the accomplishment, does not wholly fill God's vision in the Word for those He draws to Himself. Paul longed that the disciples might be: "filled with the knowledge of His will in all spiritual wisdom and understanding" (Col.1:9).

It is in this respect that the inter-denominational idea falls so far short of the divine ideal. Rejoice as we do that souls are saved, and God blesses many through inter-denominational activity. We cannot but deplore the sad confusion of teaching which is at once encountered by new converts. Our conviction is that they should be gathered together according to the one faith, to serve in Churches of God as disciples did in apostolic times. Believers separated in this way from unscriptural associations will find themselves in a small minority compared with those who favour the inter-denominational idea. The latter regard themselves as free to move around among various groups of Christians who differ widely on the doctrines they uphold, but who seek to suppress these differences in the interests of 'unity'. This unity falls far short of the New Testament unity which the apostle Paul advocated in words such as:

"so ordain I in all the churches" (1 Cor.7:17).

"we have no such custom, neither the churches of God" (1 Cor.11:16).

"Hold the pattern of sound words which thou hast heard from me" (2 Tim.1:13).

It is therefore with sadness, yet with conviction, that the Churches of God believe they must take a separated stand in collective witness and service, despite frequent misunderstanding and criticism by fellow-believers.

A Positive Ideal

Beset by the contradictions and confusion of teaching expressed in the service of many groupings of believers, some have sought the Lord's guidance as to where they may serve Him in a truly biblical liberty of spirit. Guided, we believe, by the Holy Spirit through the Word, many have been led to see the positive ideal of Churches of Go patterned according to the Scriptures. Standing in united witness, the Churches of God are persuaded they can form the rallying point towards which the Holy Spirit can constrain others who are exercised, about giving effect to the Lord's Word, and who long for rest of spirit from doctrinal compromise.

Far from taking any kind of pride in a separated stand, the Churches of God earnestly wish to make a positive appeal to fellow Christians to consider, or re-consider, very carefully the New Testament pattern of Christian service for the day in which we live; and to come alongside us in pursuing a scriptural approach to unity in a scene of sad disarray and disunity.

POSTSCRIPT

TODAY FEW BIBLE LOVERS can fail to see the 'prophetic clock' point ever more clearly to the personal return of our Lord and Saviour Jesus Christ. The exceedingly precious truth of His return to the air for His own (1 Thess.4:14-18) was one which began increasingly to impress itself on disciples of the Lord in the days of which we have been writing. It is remarkable how biblical truths of immense importance can become lost to sight over whole eras of time until there is a reviving in searching hearts by the Holy Spirit.

Then sometimes suddenly, sometimes gradually, issues long clouded become clear again. So, we believe, have the important truths been re-discovered concerning the Churches of God which have been reviewed in historical context. The past undoubtedly illumines events and circumstances of the present and the future So, while casting our eyes back in order to share with others a heritage which has proved extremely precious to the Churches of God in our day, we do well to take stock and consider the future, however short or long it may be till the Master comes.

It was in 1920 that outreach work first commenced in Nigeria and a chain of Churches of God in that land has progressively consolidated their witness. In Nigeria, as later in Burma and India, indigenous full lime servants of the Lord among the Churches have been, and still are, gifted by the Lord to His people, as has also occurred in the UK, North America and Australia. Soon after the end of the second world war a Church of God was planted near Rangoon in Burma, and subsequently a chain of Churches grew up in North Burma as a result of the message of the truth being carried north. More recently there has been encouraging growth in India in the Chennai area and in Andhra Pradesh, with promise elsewhere in that country. There the interest has mainly arisen in companies of Christian Brethren who have learned a new dimension of church truth as they have studied the doctrines taught and held among Churches of God. Assemblies have also been planted in the Philippines, Liberia, Ghana, Belgium, Kenya and Malawi.

Since the time of the second world war the Churches of God have increased in countries outside the United Kingdom and North America more than in the areas where the movement originated. It is interesting that this seems to parallel in some degree the growth of Christian witness generally in the world, with major growth taking place in African and other countries which attained independence over the last 75 years.

A Church of God was planted in Kingston, Jamaica, as a direct result of the outreach by radio broadcast from the Churches in North America. This form of outreach has been faithfully developed in recent years, not only in North America but also in the United Kingdom and in West Africa, and has stimulated much correspondence with the mailing centres of the Churches. Still the movement is a small one and, in much dependence on the Lord of the Lampstands (Rev.1-3), testimony is maintained and outreach pursued wherever resources permit and the Lord seems to direct.

No pleasure whatever is taken in separation for its own sake from the multitude of beloved fellow-members of the Body of Christ whom we hold dear in the eternal bonds of Calvary love. But before the Lord, solemn thought, all His own will answer at the coming Judgement Seat of Christ, and truth bought dearly, we reverently believe, must not be sold. We share fully with all who love His appearing, the blessed anticipation of knowing as we have been known, and of sharing the joys of that glorious place in His presence without the barriers which human failure and conflicting convictions have erected in this world.

"BEHOLD, I COME QUICKLY."

"EVEN SO, COME, LORD JESUS."

APPENDIX

THE CHURCHES OF GOD, whose re-establishment in the period 1892-94 is described in this booklet, are designated in all legal documents as 'The Churches of God in the Fellowship of the Son of God, the Lord Jesus Christ'. This is on the basis of 1 Corinthians 1:9 and distinguishes them from other bodies of Christians which have adopted the title 'Churches of God'.

We believe that it is legitimate and true to the original to translate the words of 1 Corinthians 1:9, "the Fellowship of His Son Jesus Christ our Lord". In this scripture the apostle is addressing the Church ('ecclesia') of God in Corinth, disciples who were called by God into the fellowship of His Son. The absence of the definite article in the Greek of this text, coming before the genitive ('of') is sometimes found elsewhere in the Septuagint and in the New Testament where, through the influence of Hebrew usage, the following noun (here, 'His *Son*') makes the first noun definite. Further, the definiteness of 'the fellowship together with the thought in 'of' or 'belonging to', confirms that the phrase defines the sphere where such fellowship is steadfastly observed.

This is why capital 'F' is deemed appropriate, to distinguish from such usages as in 1 John 1:7 where the Greek speaks of fellowship with' (meta) not 'the Fellowship of' as in 1 Corinthians 1:9. This sense of the passage, 'the community belonging to His Son', is observed to be present here by some modern scholars, e.g. C.K.

Barrett: "Fellowship .... can mean community (so that here the sense would be that God has called you into the community ... of Jesus Christ)". (A Commentary on the First Epistle to the Corinthians, A. & C. Clark, 1967, p.40). It is important to note that AV, RV, and RSV all translate "the fellowship of ...".

A summary of the teachings and practices of the Churches of God follows.

They believe in:

1. The plenary inspiration of Scripture. The Bible is the Word of God; it is God-breathed. Its words are living and these alone can satisfy the deep need of the souls of men (2 Tim.3:16; 2 Pet.1:20,21).

1. The Holy Trinity: Father, Son and Holy Spirit, eternally one God (Deut.6:4; Is.57:15; 2 Cor.13:14; Heb.9:14).

1. The sovereignty of God (Rom.9:10-29).

1. The total depravity of man. By the fall of man in the garden of Eden death has come through sin and has passed unto all men, for that all have sinned (Rom.3:23, 5:6-12).

1. The deity, the virgin birth, the incarnation, the perfect life and atoning death of the eternal Son of God; His resurrection and ascension (Matt.1:23, Luke 1:26-38; John 20; Acts 10:38-40; Rom.4:25).

1. The coming of the Holy Spirit to convict the world

and indwell the believer (John 14:16-17, 16:8-15; Acts 2:1-13).

1. The apostles' teaching, precisely given by the Lord and accurately preserved in the New Testament Scriptures, intended to be the form of Christian witness till the end of the present age (Heb.2:3; Acts 2:42; Rom.6:17; Jude v.3).

They believe that:

1. At the new birth, through personal acceptance of Christ as Saviour and Lord, a person becomes a child of God, and a member of the Church which is His Body, into which he is baptised in the one Spirit (John 1:12; 2 Cor.5:17; Gal.3:26,28; 1 Cor.12:13).

1. No person, born again, and therefore baptised into the Church which is the Body of Christ, can ever be lost again. Therefore the teaching of the falling away of believers, so far as eternal life is concerned, is false (John 10:27-30; 1 Cor.3:15).

1. Following conversion and the accompanying baptism in the Holy Spirit into the one Body, the Lord's command is that the disciple should then be baptised by immersion in water and received into a Church of God. Anyone seeking fellowship who is already baptised as a believer into the Name of the Father and of the Son and of the Holy Spirit, would not be re-baptised. Infant sprinkling is unacceptable as

unscriptural (Matt.28:18-20; Acts 2:41,42 10:47,48).

1. The scriptural terms 'the Church the Body' and `the Church (or Churches) of God' are not interchangeable for they do not describe the same people. All believers from Pentecost until the Lord returns are members of the Church the Body and can never be severed from it. Most are already in heaven. A Church of God is the unit of testimony in any town or village (no matter in how many companies it may meet), and is composed solely of disciples who have been baptised and added together according to the New Testament pattern, in fellowship with Churches of God worldwide. From such Churches of God erring saints may depart or be excommunicated, thus losing their place in the Church of God locally but retaining membership of the Church the Body (Eph.5:25-27; 1 Cor.1:9, 16:19; Gal.1:2; 1 Cor.5:5,13).

1. The Church the Body is not viewed in Scripture as synonymous with the House or Temple of God. In the New Testament it is the Churches of God, linked together in a fellowship of assemblies, which together comprise the House and the Temple. The existence of the House of God is presented in the New Testament as conditional on obedience. Just as a Church of God can cease to exist, so too can the House of God (Eph.2:20-22; 1 Pet.2:4-10; Heb.3:6; Rev.2:5).

1. 'Miraculous' gifts, such as speaking in tongues, belong

to the apostolic era for the purpose of confirming the New Covenant revelation. Such gifts were, we believe, then withdrawn in harmony with Old Testament precedent that miraculous powers were given to God's servants for limited periods only (e.g. Moses, Elijah, Elisha). They are not, therefore, practised in the Churches of God. The concept of a 'second blessing', marked by speaking in tongues, which believers should seek as a sign of baptism in the Holy Spirit, is seen as unscriptural. Tongues were a sign to the unbelieving, not to them that believe. God's healing today in response to prayer is thankfully recognised, but is regarded as different from miraculous 'gifts of healing' in New Testament times (Heb.2:4; 1 Cor.14:22, 12:4-11, 28-31).

1. On the subject of prophecy, the teaching of a pre-tribulation Rapture is scriptural, every believer being caught up to meet the Lord in the air, the dead in Christ being raised, and the living saints changed. All believers will stand before the Judgement Seat of Christ, each one to receive reward according to the deeds done in the body (1 Thess.4.15-18; 2 Cor.5:10; Rom.14:10-12).

1. This is followed in due course by Daniel's seventieth week of seven years in which the Antichrist, the Man of Sin, will wield Satan's power, followed by the return of the Lord Jesus Christ to the earth in judgement, and then to enter His thousand-year reign (Dan.9:24-27; Matt.24:15-31; 2 Thess.2:3-10; Rev.20:2-10).

1. Thereafter the Devil who had been bound in the abyss for a thousand years, will re-assert his power, but will be overcome and cast into the lake of fire. When this is completed, the present heaven and earth will pass away and God will bring in a new heaven and a new earth, wherein righteousness will dwell (Rev.20:7-15, 21:1-5; Is.66:22).

Activities and Government:

1. The Breaking of the Bread is held in the morning of the Lord's day. At the beginning of the assembly service, a brother goes to the table and, first for the bread and then for the wine, gives thanks, breaks or pours, then distributes for all to partake. Only those who have been baptised by immersion as disciples, and have been added to the Church are eligible to partake of the bread and wine. Brethren then offer worship and thanksgiving by the Spirit of God, through the Great High Priest over God's House, and in the heavenly sanctuary. This constitutes the holy priesthood service of the people of God. All are encouraged to say the Amen, but beyond this and the singing, sisters take no audible part in the meeting for the Breaking of the Bread, or on any other occasion when the assembly meets 'in Church'. On all such occasions sisters have their heads covered. (1 Cor.11:2-18). After the worship is over a brother may minister the Word (Acts 20:7; 1 Cor.11:20-29; Acts 2:41,42; Heb. 10:19-22; Phil.3:3; 1 Cor.14:34-38).

1. Other activities on the Lord's day may include meetings for the ministry of the Word, Sunday School and Youth work, the preaching of the gospel in the church hall, at open air venues, hospitals, old people's homes and the like, together with distribution of gospel tracts (Matt.28:18-20; 1 Thess.1:8).

1. In the Churches there is usually at least one mid-week meeting for prayer, and with it ministry of the Word or Bible study (Acts 2:42; Rom.12:12; Eph.6:18, 4:11-13).

1. By regular arrangements also, ministry conferences, gospel rallies, special outreach meetings and gatherings for young people are held, frequently on a District basis (Matt.28:18-20; Phil.1:27).

1. In every Church there are at least two overseers or elders and, wherever possible, deacons also. Overseers meet regularly for prayer and discussion, and separately with the deacons (Acts 14:23; Titus 1:5; Phil.1:1).

1. The Churches are grouped in recognised areas corresponding in principle to the groupings of New Testament Churches in Roman provinces. The overseers in each area (usually termed Districts) meet regularly for consultation, on the principle that local overseers deal with those matters in their own Church, and overseers collectively at District level with matters affecting the Churches in the District. Any matter

beyond the capacity of local overseers, or any failure on their part in judgement, would go to overseers at District level for counsel and help (2 Cor.8:1,19; Gal.1:2; 1 Pet.1:1, 5:1-4).

1. Overseers in a country may meet by arrangement. Overseers of all the Churches world-wide meet at regular intervals. By this means, unity of teaching and practice is maintained throughout all the Churches (1 Pet. 5:1-4; 2 Cor.8:19-23; 1 Cor.4:17, 11:16; Acts 15).

1. There is no system of clergy and laity. All the brethren are encouraged in the exercise of their gift. The apostle Peter described himself simply as a 'fellow elder'; the Church of God in Philippi comprised only saints, overseers and deacons (1 Cor.14:26-33; Eph.4:10-13; 1 Cor.14:40; 1 Pet.5:1; Phil.1:1).

1. There is, however, recognition of the New Testament arrangement for the Churches to give financial support to brethren who are approved in the ministry of the Word and other forms of service, and who are commended to an itinerant ministry of evangelism and teaching (Acts 13:1-3, 15:40, 16:3; 3 John 5-8).

1. The general practice in local meetings, and larger conferences, is for all ministry of the Word to be by arrangement (1 Cor.14:26-33; Rom.12:5-8).

1. The Churches thus take their stand in witness to their understanding of the whole counsel of God. As a

consequence, while they love all His children, they maintain a position of separation in divine service. For their own people, they also teach abstention from entertainment which is detrimental to the spiritual life. In contrast to present world trends, they emphasise high standards of morality. They also disapprove of the use of tobacco and the misuse of alcohol, discourage involvement in politics or military service, and stress generally the need for life and conduct to be worthy of their high calling (Acts 20:27; 2 Cor.6:14-18; Gal.2:18; 2 Tim.2:21; 1 John 2:15; 1 Cor.9:25-27).

BIBLIOGRAPHY

Many of the truths of Holy Scripture which the Churches of God believe and practise have been mentioned briefly in this history. A series of booklets has been produced which deal with these matters in greater detail. Their titles are:

- THE FAITH: OUTLINE OF SCRIPTURE DOCTRINE

- CHURCHES OF GOD: NEW TESTAMENT PATTERN

- THE HOLY SPIRIT AND THE BELIEVER

- ELDERS AND THE ELDERHOOD

- THE BREAKING OF THE BREAD

- THE BIBLE: ITS INSPIRATION AND AUTHORITY

- THE PARABLE OF THE TABERNACLE

- THE FINGER OF PROPHECY

- THE CHURCHES OF GOD: THEIR ORIGIN AND DEVELOPMENT IN THE 20TH CENTURY

Did you love *The Search for the Truth of God*? Then you should read *The Faith: Outlines of Scripture Doctrine*[1] by Hayes Press!

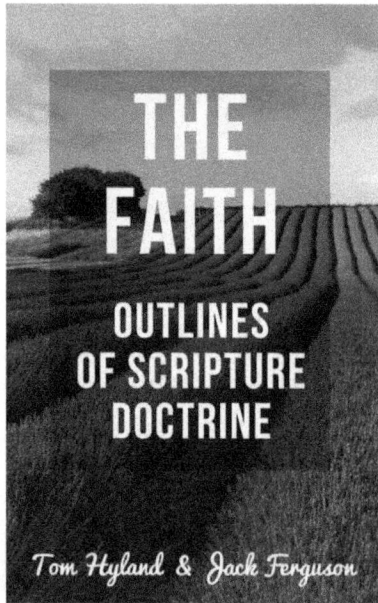

This book provides a concise outline on what the Bible has to say about 15 key doctrines or teachings of the Christian faith.

CHAPTER ONE: THE HOLY SCRIPTURES
CHAPTER TWO: THE GODHEAD
CHAPTER THREE: THE INCARNATION
CHAPTER FOUR: THE ATONEMENT
CHAPTER FIVE: THE RESURRECTION
CHAPTER SIX: ETERNAL SALVATION
CHAPTER SEVEN: THE HOLY SPIRIT

---

1. https://books2read.com/u/b5OBww

2. https://books2read.com/u/b5OBww

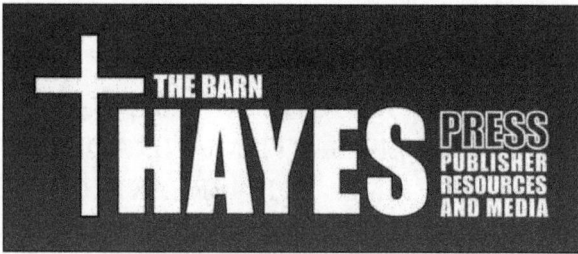

About the Publisher

Hayes Press (www.hayespress.org) is a registered charity in the United Kingdom, whose primary mission is to disseminate the Word of God, mainly through literature. It is one of the largest distributors of gospel tracts and leaflets in the United Kingdom, with over 100 titles and hundreds of thousands despatched annually. In addition to paperbacks and eBooks, Hayes Press also publishes Plus Eagles Wings, a fun and educational Bible magazine for children, and Golden Bells, a popular daily Bible reading calendar in wall or desk formats. Also available are over 100 Bibles in many different versions, shapes and sizes, Bible text posters and much more!